ENDANGERED
Sea Turtles

Bobbie Kalman

Crabtree Publishing Company

www.crabtreebooks.com

Earth's Endangered Animals Series

A Bobbie Kalman Book

Dedicated by Caroline Crabtree
To my three men—Sean, Liam, and Paul—you complete me—Love Mommy

Author and Editor-in-Chief
Bobbie Kalman

Research
Kristina Lundblad

Substantive editor
Kathryn Smithyman

Editor
Rebecca Sjonger

Design
Bobbie Kalman
Katherine Kantor
Samantha Crabtree
   (cover and title page)

Production coordinator
Heather Fitzpatrick

Photo research
Crystal Foxton

Special thanks to
South Carolina Aquarium

Consultant
Patricia Loesche, Ph.D., Animal Behavior Program,
Department of Psychology, University of Washington

Photographs
Kathy Boast - www.kathyboast.com: pages 7 (bottom), 10, 15, 21 (top)
Kathy Boast/taken at South Carolina Aquarium: page 11 (top)
Bruce Coleman Inc.: Carol Hughes: page 12; Masa Ushioda: page 19
Matthew H. Godfrey: pages 14, 20, 21 (bottom), 28, 29 (top), 30 (bottom)
Karumbe Project - Tortugas Marinas del Uruguay: page 26 (both)
Kellie Pendoley: pages 11 (bottom), 24, 25
Seapics.com: © David B. Fleetham: title page, pages 4-5; © Doug Perrine: pages 13,
   30 (top); © Mark Strickland: page 27
Other images by Creatas, Digital Stock and Digital Vision

Illustrations and artwork
Barbara Bedell: page 23 (bottom)
© Ian Coleman/colemangallery.com: pages 16-17
Katherine Kantor: page 9 (black sea turtle)
Margaret Amy Reiach: pages 3 (background), 18, 23 (top), 25
Bonna Rouse: back cover (bottom), border, pages 3 (leatherback turtle),
   7, 8, 9 (except black sea turtle), 27, 31
Tiffany Wybouw: back cover (top left and right) pages 5, 15, 22, 24

Crabtree Publishing Company

www.crabtreebooks.com   1-800-387-7650

Copyright © **2004 CRABTREE PUBLISHING COMPANY**.
All rights reserved. No part of this publication may be
reproduced, stored in a retrieval system or be transmitted in
any form or by any means, electronic, mechanical, photocopying,
recording, or otherwise, without the prior written permission
of Crabtree Publishing Company. In Canada: We acknowledge the
financial support of the Government of Canada through the Book
Publishing Industry Development Program (BPIDP) for our
publishing activities.

Cataloging-in-Publication Data
Kalman, Bobbie.
   Endangered sea turtles / Bobbie Kalman.
      v. cm. -- (Earth's endangered animals series)
Includes index.
Contents: Endangered!--What is a sea turtle?--Eight species of sea turtles--How
many are left on Earth?--Meet the ridleys!--The leatherback--Green and black sea
turtles--The hawksbill--Sea turtle habitats--Back to the beach--The life cycle of a
sea turtle--Dangers all around--Sea turtle troubles--Habitat loss--Helping sea turtles.
   ISBN 0-7787-1853-0 (RLB) -- ISBN 0-7787-1899-9 (pbk.)
   1. Sea turtles--Juvenile literature. 2. Endangered species--Juvenile literature.
[1. Sea turtles. 2. Turtles. 3. Endangered species.] I. Title.
   QL666.C536K34 2004
   597.92'8--dc22
                                                          2003027778
                                                              LC

**Published in
the United States**
PMB 16A
350 Fifth Ave.
Suite 3308
New York, NY
10118

**Published
in Canada**
616 Welland Ave.
St. Catharines, Ontario
L2M 5V6

**Published in the
United Kingdom**
White Cross Mills
Hight Town, Lancaster
LA1 4XS

**Published
in Australia**
386 Mt. Alexander Rd.
Ascot Vale (Melbourne)
VIC 3032

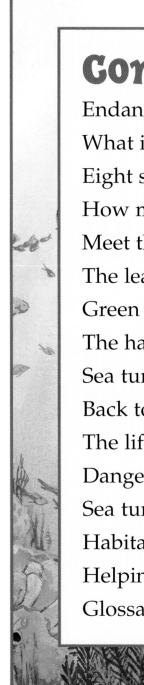

Contents

Endangered!

Sea turtles have been on Earth for at least 150 million years. Once there were millions of sea turtles living in the world's oceans, but today there are far fewer. All **species**, or types, of sea turtles are **endangered**, and some are **critically endangered**.

Animals in trouble

There are more than 1,000 known species of endangered animals on Earth today. In a few years, many species may become **extinct**. Some species of sea turtles are very close to becoming extinct. Find out more about sea turtles, such as the green sea turtles on the right, why they are endangered, and how people can help them.

Words to know

Scientists use special words to describe animals that are in danger. Read and find out what the words below mean.

extinct Describes animals that have died out and have not been seen for at least 50 years in the **wild,** or places that are not controlled by people

extinct in the wild Describes animals that survive only in zoos or other areas managed by people

critically endangered Describes animals that are at high risk of dying out in the wild

endangered Describes animals that are in danger of dying out in the natural places where they live

vulnerable Describes animals that may become endangered because they face certain dangers where they live

5

What is a sea turtle?

A sea turtle is a **reptile**. Reptiles are **cold-blooded animals**. The body temperatures of cold-blooded animals change as their surroundings change. Reptiles have backbones and scales, and they breathe air with **lungs**. Some reptiles live on land, whereas others live in water. Sea turtles are **marine reptiles**, which live only in oceans. Sea turtles must swim to the surface to breathe air.

hawksbill sea turtle

Most sea turtles have strong jaws with sharp ridges for tearing off bits of food. They have no teeth and swallow their food whole.

A sea turtle's body
Sea turtles have **streamlined**, or smoothly shaped, bodies that glide easily through water. They have two pairs of flippers that allow them to swim quickly.

Sea turtles have one or two claws on their front and back flippers. The leatherback sea turtle has no claws at all.

The top of a sea turtle's shell is called a **carapace**. The bottom of the shell is called a **plastron**. When scientists measure sea turtles, they measure the lengths of their carapaces.

plastron

carapace

a female's tail

a male's tail

You can tell if a sea turtle is male or female by its tail. The tails of males are much longer and thicker than the tails of females.

7

Eight species of sea turtles

There are more than 300 species of turtles, but there are only eight sea turtle species. They are the Kemp's ridley sea turtle, the olive ridley sea turtle, the hawksbill sea turtle, the flatback sea turtle, the black sea turtle, the loggerhead sea turtle, the green sea turtle, and the leatherback sea turtle. They are shown here from smallest to largest.

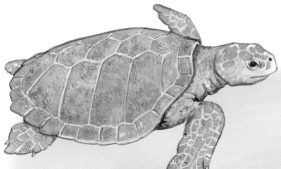

2. The olive ridley is also a small sea turtle. It is 24 to 32 inches (61-81 cm) long and weighs under 100 pounds (45 kg).

1. The Kemp's ridley is the smallest of all the sea turtles. It is about 24 inches (61 cm) long and weighs less than 100 pounds (45 kg).

4. The flatback is just over 36 inches (91 cm) long and weighs up to 200 pounds (91 kg).

3. The hawksbill is up to 36 inches (91 cm) long and weighs over 100 pounds (45 kg).

8

5. The black sea turtle measures up to 39 inches (99 cm) long and weighs as much as 220 pounds (100 kg).

6. The loggerhead is 32 to 41 inches (81-104 cm) long and weighs up to 350 pounds (159 kg).

7. The green sea turtle measures up to 48 inches (1.2 m) in length and weighs 300 to 400 pounds (136 to 181 kg).

8. The leatherback is the largest sea turtle. It can grow to a length of eight feet (2.4 m) and can weigh 1,400 pounds (635 kg).

How many are left on Earth?

Sea turtles spend most of their lives at sea, but the females swim to sandy beaches to **nest**. They nest by digging holes in the sand and laying eggs in the holes. When people count the number of sea turtles that are alive, they count the nesting females. Scientists do not count male sea turtles because they rarely leave the ocean. It is difficult to count the total number of sea turtles around the world, so the numbers you see in this book may not be exact. Scientists do know, however, that each year there are fewer nesting sea turtles in most places, and that all sea turtles are endangered.

Sea turtles leave the ocean to nest. Sometimes they also come out of the water to warm themselves on sunny beaches.

The loggerhead

The loggerhead is named for its very large head. It feeds on clams, lobsters, shrimp, and crabs by crushing these animals with its powerful jaws. Loggerheads live throughout the world, as far north as Canada and as far south as Chile. There are fewer than 60,000 nesting loggerhead females left on Earth.

The flatback

The flatback is named after its flat shell. This sea turtle lives only in ocean waters near Australia and Papua New Guinea. It has the smallest **range** of any sea turtle. Range is the area in which an animal lives and travels. There are fewer than 7,500 flatback nesting females left in the world. Flatbacks are endangered, but there is not enough information to know if they are critically endangered.

11

Meet the ridleys!

The Kemp's ridley

The Kemp's ridley is named after Richard Kemp, the fisherman who helped discover and study it. Kemp's ridleys live mainly in the Gulf of Mexico, but some have traveled as far north as Canada. They are critically endangered sea turtles. There are fewer than 1,000 nesting females in the world today! The main reason that these sea turtles are so endangered is that humans and animals eat their eggs. Besides having their eggs eaten, as shown in the picture above, Kemp's ridleys also face many of the dangers faced by other sea turtles. (See pages 24-29.)

The olive ridley

The olive ridley sea turtle is named for its olive-colored shell. This endangered sea turtle lives in the Pacific, Atlantic, and Indian Oceans. There are about 800,000 nesting females in the world. Most swim to certain beaches to nest in groups that may include hundreds of sea turtles! These huge nesting events are called *arribadas*, from a Spanish word *arribar*, which means "to arrive." During many *arribadas*, local people are allowed to collect some of the turtle eggs. Often, however, almost all the eggs laid by the sea turtles are collected.

When too many eggs are collected by people during arribadas *such as this one, few eggs are left to* **hatch** *into baby olive ridleys.*

The leatherback

Other sea turtles have shells, but the leatherback does not. Instead, it has a ridged rubbery back. Leatherbacks live in oceans all over the world, and they are critically endangered everywhere. In the Pacific Ocean, there are only 2,300 nesting females still alive. Worldwide, there are about 34,000 nesting females, but few of the eggs laid by these sea turtles will ever hatch. In some places, almost all the eggs are eaten by people and animals. The leatherback is also endangered because of the food it eats. Leatherbacks have very weak jaws, so sea jellies are their favorite meal. Sea jellies are easy to swallow whole. Tragically, leatherbacks often choke on plastic bags and balloons, which they mistake for sea jellies.

Green and black sea turtles

Most scientists agree that green sea turtles and black sea turtles are separate species. For many years, however, they were believed to be the same species. Both species are endangered.

Green sea turtles

Green sea turtles are named for the green-colored fat under their shells. There are about 203,000 nesting females left. Green sea turtles are killed for their meat and fat, which are used to make turtle soup. Another reason that green sea turtles are endangered is that **pollution** kills the sea grasses on which they feed. If there is less grass, there is less food to eat.

Black sea turtles

The black sea turtle looks just like the green sea turtle above, but its shell is almost black, and its head is smaller. There are fewer than 10,000 black sea turtles left. Like green sea turtles, black sea turtles are caught for their meat, but they are also captured for their **hides**, or skins, which are used to make leather gift items.

The hawksbill

The hawksbill sea turtle is named for the shape of its jaw, which looks like a hawk's beak. This critically endangered sea turtle lives in the Pacific, Indian, and Atlantic Oceans. In the last 30 years, more than 50,000 hawksbills have been killed for their shells, and the killing continues. Items made from **tortoiseshell**, or polished turtle shell, are popular in Japan, Italy, and Germany. So many hawksbills are being killed to make tortoiseshell objects, that only about 8,000 nesting females are left in the whole world! Not only are adults at risk, but baby hawksbills are also killed and stuffed as ornaments.

Sea turtle habitats

A **habitat** is the natural place in which a plant or an animal lives. The sea turtle's main habitat is the ocean, but beaches are also important to sea turtles because that is where they lay their eggs. Sea turtles live in warm waters throughout the oceans of the world. They live only in salt water.

Most sea turtles live and find food in shallow waters near shorelines. They swim among **coral reefs**, in **lagoons**, and in areas that are rich in seaweeds and sea grasses. Leatherbacks are the only sea turtle species that live mainly in the deep cold waters far out in the ocean.

These green sea turtles are swimming in shallow water, where they find plenty of sea grasses to eat.

What do sea turtles eat?

Different species of sea turtles have different diets. Most sea turtles are **carnivores**. They eat fish, crabs, sponges, and sea cucumbers. They also eat fish eggs. Green sea turtles eat mostly sea grasses, but they also eat small shellfish and sponges. Leatherbacks eat mainly sea jellies. Hawksbills, shown above, prefer sponges, but they also eat other sea animals such as coral.

Back to the beach

Sea turtles live in the ocean, but adult females go ashore to nest. They do not nest on just any beach, however. Each female swims to the beach where she hatched from an egg. Some females swim thousands of miles to nest! When a sea turtle arrives at a beach, she pulls herself across the sand to find a spot where she can dig an **egg chamber**, or a hole into which she lays her eggs. She sweeps away the sand with her front flippers and digs the hole with her back flippers. Depending on the species, a female turtle lays a **clutch** of 50 to 180 soft-shelled eggs, as shown below. She may nest four times during a season.

Back to the sea

When the sea turtle has finished laying her eggs, she covers them with sand and drags herself back to the ocean. Most sea turtles nest at night, but they know how to find their way back in the dark. The sky looks brighter over water, so they head toward the light. Many beaches have hotels with bright lights, however, causing some sea turtles to go the wrong way.

The green sea turtle above and the leatherback below are returning to the ocean after nesting.

The life cycle of a sea turtle

Every animal goes through a **life cycle**. A life cycle is made up of all the changes that happen to an animal from the time it is born or hatches from an egg to the time it becomes an adult that can make babies of its own.

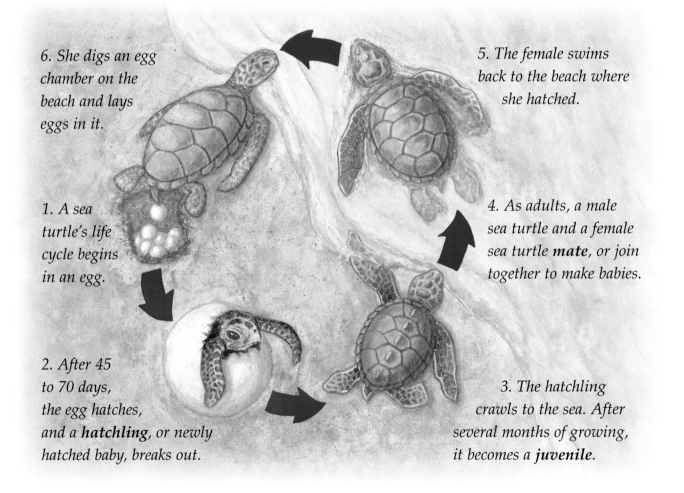

6. She digs an egg chamber on the beach and lays eggs in it.

1. A sea turtle's life cycle begins in an egg.

*2. After 45 to 70 days, the egg hatches, and a **hatchling**, or newly hatched baby, breaks out.*

5. The female swims back to the beach where she hatched.

*4. As adults, a male sea turtle and a female sea turtle **mate**, or join together to make babies.*

*3. The hatchling crawls to the sea. After several months of growing, it becomes a **juvenile**.*

Life inside the egg

After a sea turtle has laid her eggs, the sand **incubates** them, or keeps them warm. Each egg contains an **embryo** and a **yolk sac**. The embryo is the growing baby, and the yolk sac is its food. When the embryo is fully formed, it is ready to hatch.

embryo

yolk sac

Breaking out

The hatchling uses its **egg tooth** to break the egg's shell. It then pushes its way out of the egg and moves its flippers quickly to dig itself out of the egg chamber. It can take a hatchling several days to reach the surface of the sand! From there, it crawls to the ocean.

Dangers all around

A baby does not hatch from every sea turtle egg. **Predators** such as coyotes, raccoons, wild dogs, and especially people, may take sea turtle eggs from the nests. Sometimes not a single egg is left! Even if some babies do hatch, they face many dangers on the beach. They must make their way to the ocean. The journey is a long one! Sea turtles do not move easily or quickly on land. They are easy targets for predators such as crabs and birds, which grab them as they cross the beach.

Not enough babies

Sea turtles usually do not start making babies until they are over 25 years old. A female then lays eggs only every two to three years. Even though she lays several clutches of eggs in a season, very few of the eggs end up as adults that will make babies. When not enough babies hatch, the **population**, or number of sea turtles, gets smaller and smaller.

Sea turtle troubles

(above) This sea turtle became tangled in a net and is being freed by the people who found it. (below) Back into the sea it goes!

Baby sea turtles that do reach the ocean face the same dangers as those faced by adult sea turtles. Some are captured by hunters, and others get tangled in floating **debris**, or garbage. Floating debris harms living things in the ocean, including sea turtles.

Fishing nets

Many sea turtles are also caught in fishing nets. When a sea turtle is stuck in a fishing net, it cannot rise to the surface to breathe. Shrimp **trawl nets** are especially dangerous to sea turtles. Each year, thousands of sea turtles die in these fishing nets.

26

Illegal hunters

Poachers are people who kill animals and sell their body parts **illegally**. Poachers kill sea turtles for their shells, fat, and meat. Many poachers also collect sea turtle eggs. Sea turtle shells are made into souvenirs, and sea turtle meat and eggs are used as food. They are also used to make medicines in Asian countries.

Pollution

Sea turtles are harmed by pollution as well. Pollution is caused when oil and other chemicals are dumped into oceans. Pollution causes terrible diseases in sea turtles. Thousands of sea turtles die as a result of these diseases.

(above) Sea turtle eggs are sold in markets in countries such as Indonesia.

27

Habitat loss

These tourists are disturbing a leatherback turtle that is laying eggs.

The greatest threat to all sea turtles is **habitat loss**. Habitat loss is the destruction of the natural areas in which animals live, feed, or nest. Not only are the oceans of the world being polluted, but homes, hotels, and restaurants are being built on beaches where sea turtles nest. Nesting females are frightened away by people. Sea turtles sometimes leave without covering the eggs they have laid. The eggs are then crushed by cars, golf carts, or tourists walking on the beach.

28

Problems on land

When hundreds of people use the beaches where sea turtles nest, they cause big problems for sea turtles.

• When there is **erosion** on beaches, people put up walls or place sandbags on the beaches to stop the sand from washing away. Sea turtles cannot climb over these obstacles to find dry nesting areas.

• Sometimes construction companies take sand from beaches. When sea turtles lay eggs on these beaches, they cannot bury their eggs deeply enough. The eggs are then washed away by **tides**.

• Both nesting sea turtles and hatchlings are confused by artificial lights coming from buildings, and they head toward the lights instead of the ocean. When sea turtles go the wrong way, they often die.

• Raking beaches with machines can **compact**, or pack together, sand so much that hatchlings cannot dig their way out of a nest. Hatchlings may also find it hard to crawl out of the ruts left by the wheels of beach-cleaning machines.

• Sea turtles cannot nest on beaches that are full of tourists and cluttered with objects, such as the beach on the right.

(above) Large objects such as sandbags are difficult or impossible for sea turtles to cross as they search for nesting places.

29

Helping sea turtles

People all over the world are working hard to save sea turtles. They help these animals in several ways.

Safe beaches

Conservationists are people who provide animals with safe places to live and to make babies. They dig up sea turtle eggs and move them to beaches where the eggs are protected. Once the eggs hatch and the babies get bigger, the sea turtles are released back into the wild.

(above left) Volunteers are covering sea turtle egg chambers with netting to protect them from flies. The wire mesh cages under the netting help keep out predators that eat sea turtle eggs. (left) This leatherback is being tagged so scientists can count it and find out whether the sea turtle will nest again.

Escape from nets

Fishing nets kill thousands of sea turtles. Laws have been passed in many places to make fishers use special nets that have **turtle-excluding devices**, or TEDs, attached. A TED works like an escape door. Sea turtles can swim out through a TED if they are caught in a net.

Hotels helping out

Many hotels post signs that give people instructions on what to do if they see a sea turtle on a beach. At some nesting beaches, there are laws that require hotels to switch off lights during nesting seasons so sea turtles won't get confused as they head back to the ocean.

How you can help

You can help sea turtles by asking your parents not to use harsh cleaners in your home or **pesticides** on your lawn. All these chemicals end up in oceans and hurt the animals that live there. Never let helium balloons escape because they can end up in oceans and choke sea turtles. If you are ever on a beach where sea turtles nest, do not go near them and tell others to stay away as well. Pick up any discarded plastic bottles or bags on the beach so they will not be washed into the ocean.

Start surfing!

The more you know about sea turtles, the more you can help others learn why these animals are endangered. To learn more, check out these websites:

- **www.cccturtle.org/contents.htm**
- **www.seaturtleinc.com/turtles.html**
- **www.nationalgeographic.com/ngkids/9911/turtle**

Glossary

Note: Boldfaced words that are defined in the text may not appear in the glossary. The definitions on page 5 are based on the IUCN-The World Conservation Union's Red List of Threatened Species.

carnivore An animal that eats other animals

clutch A set of eggs laid at one time

coral reef A ridge or mound in the ocean made up of living coral and coral skeletons

egg tooth A small tooth used to break out of a shell

erosion The wearing or washing away of the Earth's surface by rain, wind, or water

hatch To break out of an egg

illegally Carried out against the law

juvenile Young; not yet an adult

lagoon A shallow area at the edge of an ocean, which is partly enclosed and sheltered by rocks or coral reefs

lungs Organs in the chests of animals, which are used to breathe oxygen from air

pesticide A chemical that is made to kill insects

pollution The dirty or harmful condition of water, air, or soil

predators Animals that hunt and kill other animals for food

tide The changing level of the water in oceans

trawl net A large fishing net that is dragged along the sea floor by a boat

Index

3 4 5 6 7 8 9 0   Printed in the U.S.A.   3 2 1 0 9 8 7 6